WEBSITES THAT WIN

11 Mistakes You Don't Know You're Making

By Ian Rogers

WEBSITES THAT WIN:
11 Mistakes You Don't Know You're Making

ISBN: 978-1517005634

Printed in the United States of America

First Edition

www.mvestormedia.com

This book would not have been possible without the support of these amazing people.

Michelle Cadiz
Thank you to Michelle, my fiancee, for your support in this ongoing project. You always have my back.

Brodie Tyler
Brodie, thank you for your ideas, support, encouragement, and feedback on this book! Thank you to your team of skilled writers and editors for helping me complete this.

Gordon S. Hale
Gordon, thank you for your great ideas, inspiration, conversations, and support!

KC Fong and Kathleen Stimmel
KC and Kathleen, thank you for your excellent combined design expertise in designing the cover.

Contents

Introduction

I am very excited to share this information with you. Not only is web design and development my profession, it is also my passion. Ever since I can remember, I have had a keen interest in technology. This naturally flowed to the web. Needless to say, I was the kid in high school who had his own website. This passion eventually turned into a career. I have always loved sharing ideas, so what better way to share information than through a book?

Who This Book is For

I wrote this book with the small business owner or marketing manager in mind. To be specific, any of the following would get tremendous value out of the pages to come:

- Healthcare (doctors, dentists, chiropractors, etc.)

- Contractors (general contractors, home builders, roofers, etc.)
- Professional services (accountants, attorneys, consultants, etc.)
- Business-to-business operations

The goal of this book is to better prepare business owners for the journey ahead in building a website. However, this book will not cover *how* to build a website, as your time is better spent on your profession, not learning HTML. Just as I would not perform my own dental care, a dentist should not build his own website. This book will give you tools, concepts, and ideas to make educated decisions before, during, and after the website creation process.

If you already have a website, that is okay. If it was working for you, you probably wouldn't be reading this book. The same concepts in this book can be applied to existing websites in order to improve them.

I have come across many clients who have had websites which weren't working for them. The goal of any small business and informational site should be to educate your visitors and establish leads through that education. This book will help you establish the right offers for your visitors so you can hopefully convert them into leads.

What's Not in This Book?

If you are looking to build an online store with thousands of products, this book won't cover that area. Large scale eCommerce businesses are a speciality which I do not have a lot of experience with. Although, many principles in this book may apply, specifics of eCommerce, buying behavior, and buyer psychology aren't covered.

Enjoy The ride!

To get the most out of this book, I highly recommend you **download our PDF of the Website Worksheet**. Don't worry, it's not a test or quiz. I'm not going to ask you to write pages and pages of content. This worksheet is a simple guide that will allow you to jot down ideas and retain information. You can then give that worksheet to your web designer, which will help them help you create a great website!

Most of all, enjoy! I hope you learn something along the way!

Get the Website Worksheet at
www.mvestormedia.com/book

Chapter 1

Content Is King

Mistake: Website owners don't have a plan for their content before they start their website.

So, you want to design a website. Websites are very important, as they are the center of every successful business and the prime target for getting your name, brand, or organization out there! Most people jump into the beginning stages of creating their websites thinking, "I already know what I want," and my goal is to get you to rethink that! If you already knew what you wanted, you wouldn't be reading this!

Your website will boil down to a few important things, the first being content. What does *content* mean to you?

Planning content for your website is crucial. It will be the road map for your entire site, and because it's so important you will first need a plan. And *then* a design. The plan/design will ultimately help you reach your business goals, outside of your website. You wouldn't begin building a house without a blueprint, right? Of course not!

The Beginning of the End... Result

You first need to understand *why* and for *whom* you are creating a website. You start by defining your target market and buyer personas—that is, figure out who is searching for what your business is selling.

What *is* a **buyer persona**, you ask? A buyer persona, according to HubSpot, is "a semi-fictional representation of your ideal customer based on market research and real data about your existing customers."

The layout of your website is very important; information needs to be structured. If you structure your site navigation to represent your buyer personas, you'll get a much better site right off the bat. You want your content to be meaningful to your *users*, not to yourself. I'll cover navigation and layout in more detail in chapter 6, and content in chapter 9.

Content boils down to how you structure it and present it. Once you have the content right, that will determine the navigation, and once you have the navigation, your design team can then build the design.

This is why it is so critical to get the content, or road map if you will, done first.

Keep in mind, site structure shouldn't be boring! Your website should immediately draw your users' attention and please them both visually and emotionally.

We've all been there...we are in the heat of our search, we click on a website, and BAM! Our brains immediately seize up.

The site is neither pleasing to the eye nor easy to navigate, and it takes us less than five seconds to hit that "back" button. We will help you set yourself apart!

Let's Talk Navigation...

If I could mention one key piece of knowledge, it would be to build your website design around your content, not the content around your design! I can't stress enough how crucial this is.

This is why all the content you create should be based on your target market and buyer personas. Study the primary qualities of each specifically designed target market to get a better sense of who you're trying to reach, and make sure your website addresses these key points in order to attract the right or qualified people.

Attracting qualified people to your website saves

you time and money. I'll go into the reasons why later.

So, what *is* a target market?

"A particular group of consumers at which a product or service is aimed."

Thank you, Mr. Webster; I couldn't agree more. I'd like to emphasize the *aimed* part.

So, in simple terms, content that is specifically created for your target market will cater to the individuals you are trying to attract most while weeding out the others.

This is a very important advantage, as time is of more value than money, am I right?

> **A brilliant side note:** the content you create *specifically* for people in your target market becomes more meaningful and beneficial to them. It resonates with them: *This is exactly what I need; this answers my questions.*

Another great reason to tailor content to your target market is that it allows you to determine and then create content based on the different stages of the sales process.

Those individuals looking for more information regarding your services or what you offer are probably more likely to go to your FAQs section. That's a no-brainer!

But those who understand what they're looking for and have already determined that *you* are what they need will head for your pricing section.

These consumers are evaluating their vendors. They single out the ones that draw their attention, make it easy to navigate through what they want to find, and provide clear and concise information on what the vendor offers and how much it will "hit them where it hurts"!

Now that we've covered that, let's get a better understanding of your buyer personas.

Buyer Personas: Not the Mythical Creatures They Appear to Be.

By defining your buyer personas, you can customize your sales process and the information on your website. Instead of using generic titles on your website like "about me," you can customize these categories to suit your buyer personas.

Take, for example, an attorney who has a practice that focuses on three key legal services that prospective buyer personas (or clients) may need:

- personal injury
- criminal defense
- traffic tickets

The attorney can customize each section of the website to specifically cater to clients who would need that service. Now we're getting somewhere!

This is much more beneficial than just throwing a general "services" tab on your navigation bar, right?

Don't get me wrong; it's still beneficial to provide sections for general information like pricing and FAQs, as well as any other relevant information that might help you qualify your buyer.

Let's share an example. Here are two different buyer personas, [buyer personas should be fictional people with real names to help build your precise target market.] Our two examples are Procrastinating Patty and Overachiever Andy.

Procrastinating Patty

She was so excited to get to work one day that Procrastinating Patty got herself a little speeding ticket. Bummer. But instead of taking care of the problem immediately, she took her sweet time and missed resolving this dilemma. Now she needs an attorney, STAT.

Procrastinating Patty has found your website because she sees that you offer a same-day court appearance service, and she needs you *right now*. See where am I going with this?

Having a designated tab for this same-day court

appearance service that was readily available to your buyer persona just landed you a new client. Don't make them look for it.

Patty realizes that her procrastination has cost her that hot new pair of Jimmy Choos she's had her eye on, but you're keeping her out of the slammer, and for that, she's thankful...because she doesn't look good in stripes.

As an added bonus, making your services and pricing available on your website gave Patty what she needed ASAP. That won her over, as she didn't have to spend time searching to find out how broke she was about to be...and let's be real here, *ain't nobody got time for mindless searching!*

Are you beginning to see why defining your target audience and your buyer personas plays a massive role in the design of your website? It weeds out your unqualified prospects and helps bring you qualified ones.

One More for the Win!

Since you created your website around the goods and services you provide, so clients can see them up front, you have potentially inherited another buyer persona:

Overachiever Andy

Overachiever Andy happens to be Procrastinating

Patty's BFF. Cute, right? And because she raved about how amazing you were, he thinks he had better check you out, just in case he gets himself a little ticket down the road. See where this is going? The better you are, the more people are going to talk about you!

Winning!

So, Then What?

Now that you've been thinking about all your possible buyer personas, your initial thoughts on your website design have probably changed. Or at least, I hope they have!

> Write down a few qualifying factors of your target market in your Website Worksheet. Try to organize them into groups or personas.

At this point, I recommend using a site organizational chart called a sitemap—a map that allows you to build one exceptional and highly sought-after website for all your personas.

Try to think about what those personas might want to click on, what major categories they would be looking for. Let this generate the content that successfully structures your site.

Okay, So How Do I Do That?

Now that you've learned what buyer personas are

and you've soaked in the benefits of what a sitemap can do for your design process, you can get started on creating your very own sitemap!

Take a minute to define your potential personas, and then use the example below to create a sitemap that will list all the relevant sections you wish to have on your website, as well as the potential content each section (or tab) will house.

If you are feeling a bit more daring, click the link below and download our free sitemap to get you started!

Use the chart in the Website Worksheet to create a sitemap of your website, based on your target market and buyer personas.

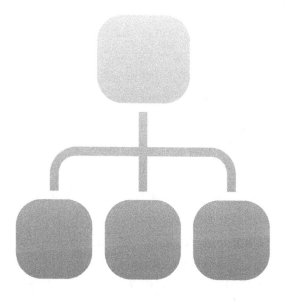

And Now That I've Created a Sitemap?

Once you have your layout, you can generate website traffic and more potential leads by building calls-to-action. Ideally, each section on your site should have one.

A call-to-action (usually abbreviated as CTA) is an image or line of text that prompts your visitors, leads, and customers to take action. It is, quite literally, a "call" to take an "action." — HubSpot

Pretty simple, right?

Your call-to-action can be relatively straightforward; don't over-think things! It can take the form of an opt-in, a phone number, or a form to fill out. The more specific your call-to-action is to a particular section, the better.

For example, personas that are still in the early stages of their journeys would benefit from a newsletter or eBook opt-in with more information on your goods or services. It eliminates the pressure to buy but gives your visitors a small amount of information to help move them along in their decision. Think of this as a "teaser," if you will.

Also keep in mind that you don't want to push your visitors to buy *all the time*. That's the fastest way to lose a potential lead. Trust me—think about how annoying a pushy salesman is. When your customers are ready to buy, they will. Or they won't, but either way, you have refrained from being the pushy sales troll. No one likes a troll.

And That's a Wrap!

Well, that pretty much covers the chapter 1 basics! Chapter 2 is going to head things up a bit with the proper use of domain names. See you there!

Chapter 2

Domain Names

Mistake: Using a domain name no one can take seriously

As you may have already guessed, this chapter will cover domain names. Clever, huh?

So, what *is* a domain name? Pretty self-explanatory really, but your domain name represents your company and should be taken very seriously.

When you're using your domain name to market your business, there are a couple of things you need to take into consideration, because your domain name is on *everything*: your business cards, print collateral, social media sites, and even email address.

Speaking of email addresses—you want people to see your company as legit, right? Then you don't want to be using an @gmail or @AOL type of email address. You're not twelve, and neither is your company... unless of course your business is in fact twelve years old, in which case you should already have an established, non gmail or AOL email address. I highly recommend using your domain name for your business's email.

Many of you reading this book already have a domain name. You're one step ahead of the game, so feel free to skip to the next chapter!

For the rest of you, this chapter is going to cover the standards and best practices for getting and using a domain name.

So let's get started!

How Do I choose a Domain Name?

Getting a domain name is relatively easy; at Mvestor Media, we recommend using GoDaddy.com to set up all new domain name purchases. They really are the go-to domain name masters. They also don't overcharge for them.

There are others, but honestly, GoDaddy is one of—if not the—best. Simple, efficient, effective. The website is user friendly, and it makes finding a name easy. You can punch in yourcompanyname.com, and it will give you results for pretty much all the names that are available for the top-level domains.

Standard Top-Level Domains (TLDs)

Here is a list of the widely available TLDs that your organization can use, based on what type of enterprise you are—or will be—running. The TLD is what comes after the "dot" - .com, .net etc.

- .com is for commercial and/or business use. It is also the most widely used domain.

- .org is typically for non-profit organizations.

- .net was originally for network providers but is more commonly used as a backup if the .com you wanted isn't available.

- .info is typically used for informational services.

- .biz is for business services.

The following TLDs are ones that require prior approval in order to obtain.

- .mil is for military organizations.

- .edu is used by educational organizations (post-high school).

- .gov is for government agencies.

Ideally, you want to choose a domain name that will represent you as the business owner and, like-wise, choose the correct TLD to use for all marketing and email purposes.

Once you have your domain name with TLD in place, you'll want to take the next, very important, step to protect it by securing all the other TLDs as well (.com, .org, .net, .info, .biz, .us). For example, if your domain name is Widgets.com, it would be smart to secure Widgets.net, Widgets.org, Widgets.info, and so on. If you don't, someone else could buy one and "hold it hostage," and you'd end up paying through the nose if you decided you wanted the rights to it! Don't go crazy here, though; the first few TLDs are probably enough.

New Top-Level Domains

Today, new TLDs are being introduced, such as

- .vegas
- .construction
- .guru
- .club
- .reviews
- .services

In my humble opinion, they're kind of ridiculous. Now that the internet is booming, .com domain names are harder to come by, so people are either creating domain names that are longer—which isn't helpful because people will never remember those ridiculously long domain names—or they're using these newer TLDs.

On the other hand, if any of the newer TLDs actually pertain to you, feel free to purchase them—just don't get caught up securing *all* of them. That's thousands of dollars that could be spent elsewhere...like on your website.

Plus, the value of these new TLDs diminishes fairly quickly, because more TLDs are introduced each month.

Keep in Mind...

Your main goal is to use a standard, traditional TLD—either .com, .org, or .net—to represent your website, for professional reasons. These newer TLDs are not yet mainstream and will obviously take some time to become widely used and accepted. This is another area where the legitimacy factor comes into play.

Now let's cover some best practices, shall we?

Best Practices

When you're choosing a domain name, keep in mind: the shorter the better (for example, Widgets. com). If the shortest domain isn't available, you can try your business's legal name. This shows you're incorporated and/or legitimate. (for example, WidgetsInc.com).

Should neither of those be available, you can also try using your city or state. Ideally, just one or the other (for example, WidgetsNY.com or WidgetsCA. com).

I want to stress that the simpler your company name is, the better. It's easier for people to remember and type into their search engines if there aren't 239,475,293 characters.

A few more key points/suggestions:

- Domain names are not case-sensitive. Registration includes both uppercase and lowercase versions.

- If possible, buy common misspellings of your company name and redirect them to your main site to avoid losing potential visitors. (You don't need to go crazy with this, though.)

- When you buy your domain, you don't need to purchase all the upsell items, such as search engine optimization, privacy, and web hosting (chapter 11 will cover finding a good web host). Just buy the domain name.

- Make sure you pay your bill, and don't ignore those renewal notices. This is very important! You only have about a two-week window to address those, otherwise everyone else has the opportunity to buy your domain and hold it hostage if you want it back. Losing your domain name can be very costly, so know when your stuff is going to renew! This includes all the important dates for your hosting company, too! They will wipe out your site, and there isn't a backup!

- Put renewal dates on your calendar.
- Keep your credit card info up to date.
- Make sure your billing is in order.
- Ensure that each company has your current address and phone numbers.
- Make sure you're receiving emails and other correspondence from your web host and registrar.

Last, But Not Least: The Long Term

Typically, a registrar will offer discounts if you plan to register for multiple years up front. If this website is going to be around a while, it would be wise to pay more up front for more years rather than going through the hassle of re-registering it every single year.

It may be more expensive up front, but your price per year will be lower. It's a win-win.

Use the Website Worksheet to write down possible domain name options for your website.

Chapter 3

Visitors First

Mistake: Creating a website with you in mind and not your visitors.

Moving right along—we're diving into the good stuff, now! This chapter will discuss how to create a website that provides exceptional customer service. How do you get it, how do you use it, and how do you make it exceptional?

Start by asking, "How important is customer service to me?"

In a perfect world, every business and all departments within it would work in glorious harmony to ensure that every customer was satisfied, content, and happy, right? And I rode my unicorn to work today. Let's look at the harsh reality of customer service: ridiculous waiting times, 50 million different numbers to push just to speak to a human, and 40 million transfers to "someone who knows more," just to be disconnected in the end. Such a waste of time.

At Mvestor Media, we want to change that. Your website is a direct reflection of the customer service *you* want to provide. Saying, "We value customer service" doesn't count. You have to say what you mean and mean what you say. Fascinating concept, right? Wouldn't it be great if *every* company followed those principles?

Well, we can only do our small parts in this uphill battle, and it begins with you!

Customer Service: Does Your Website Make the Grade?

Ask yourself, how is your website going to provide content that your visitors can expect to find? How you go about building your website, and how you treat your customers on your site, is a direct reflection of how you value customer service. Deep, right?

> **Example:** When you introduce new services or products, you usually want feedback on them. Use your website as a tool to gather that information and use it your advantage, making changes to your business process or products in order to deliver the best possible solution to your customers. Make sure your site serves your audience's needs.

I'm not saying that you necessarily need to provide a "live chat" option on your website, but you want your customers or prospects to have a good experience on your site, just like you want them to have a good experience using your product or service.

What Matters on a Website?

C-O-N-T-R-O-L! Am I right, ladies?

Okay, I don't mean that just for the ladies...but you want your visitors to have *complete* control when they come to your site, because as soon as you take control away from them, i.e. redirect them in some form, they get frustrated and will most likely leave your site.

This goes with the modern web as a whole. Take away control from a user, they take themselves away from you.

We've all been there. We search the internet for something we want, scour countless websites to try and find it, and then click on a website that navigationally won't allow us to go where we want. What do we do? We hit the back button.

When your visitors or current customers come to your website in search of something, give it to them! And by all means, *don't be shady*. Don't hide your phone number; don't make it hard for someone to get a hold of you. Likewise, don't hide your email address.

Client feedback is your best source of *honest* information. When you're looking to make improvements or changes, you should heavily weigh client critiques, so don't make it hard for clients to talk to you!

Also, don't make *all* your website's external resource links open in a new window or tab. When you do this, you take away the users' ability to use the "back" button. If your users want to stay on your site, they will, but forcing them to will only frustrate them. Why? Because you took away their control. We all like to be in control, even in the slightest, less noticeable ways!

And above all, avoid unsolicited pop-ups or annoying opt-ins. Not all pop-ups are "bad" per se... but pop-ups can be annoying, and they interrupt whatever your visitors were reading, searching for, or purchasing. Steer clear of pop-ups unless your visitors are asking for them. (By that I mean, if your user *clicks* on something and it pops up, that's okay.)

If visitors aren't asking for certain information, don't just make it pop up arbitrarily out of nowhere. The users need to have control, period. When they don't, they get mad and run. (Not literally, but you get my point.)

Make Your Content Readable

Without a doubt, everyone who has a website wants to rank on the first page, if not the first spot, on Google. Yes, this is important—very important—but

> **Other good reads:** This book isn't going to cover all things Google and marketing, but **_Inbound Marketing_** by Brodie Tyler does. I suggest you get yourself a copy in order to better understand how Google will one day rule the planet. Of course, I'm kidding about ruling the planet... sort of. But seriously, buy the book—you won't be disappointed.
>
> Back in 2005, Steve Krug wrote another great book, titled **_Don't Make Me Think_**, and it rings true to this day. Though it was originally written for web designers, business owners who want their users to have the best experience on their sites will benefit from it too.
>
> Pick up a copy of both these great books!

making sure your content is readable is much more important.

How does website readability relate to customer service? Let me explain. It's assumed that inserting "**_keywords_**" into your content will show Google and other search engines that your content is more relevant than other pages on the web. But while creating copy *around* keywords is very helpful, content that is just stuffed with keywords becomes overbearing and irrelevant to your reader.

If you prioritize keywords over readability, it means your visitor is of secondary importance to a search engine. That's not good, because search engines have the capability to understand that you're doing this and can penalize your site by not ranking you at all. No matter what you've been told, or what you hear, never do anything specifically *for* Google. The programmers are smart. They will figure it out.

The paradox is that the best way to rank in the search engine King, is, among other things, to focus your efforts on making sure that the user has a good experience.

It all comes down to the experience!

So What Does This All Mean?

Your site will rank higher based on your customers' and visitors' *experience*. Keep customer service as a priority, and work diligently to provide your users with exactly what they're looking for, as well as 100 percent control in getting it. The less your users have to think, the better their experience on your site is going to be! Sad, right?

Make your copy quick and easy to read. Your visitors are "skimmers," and they won't be digesting every inch of your page. They will be driving through your site at 90 miles per hour, so your "billboard" had better catch their attention fast!

Just remember, people love to design their sites based on their own bias, rather than asking themselves, "What's best for my visitors?" Your site shouldn't be designed based on "*I* want this" or "*I* want that."

I can best summarize this chapter by saying, *take your customers' needs into account when creating your website.*

Using the information from this chapter, use the Website Worksheet to implement a customer service policy for your website.

Chapter 4

Think Mobile: It's Where It's At!

Mistake: Building a website that's not mobile friendly.

In 2014, 79.1 percent of the global online population accessed the internet from mobile phones. That's an increase of 5.7 percent from the previous year's users. Those numbers are staggering, and they're only projected to climb in the coming years.

Look around you—how many people are on their phones right now? Nearly *everyone*. The number of people who still access web content from a desktop PC is rapidly dwindling, as the new wave of technology is centered around *everything* being mobile.

People check their email, shop, talk, text, and even plan out their days from their phones, tablets, or other devices.

Let that sink in for a minute, because what I'm about to cover just might blow your mind. It's also likely to throw a wrench into the design plan you *thought* you had already figured out.

Constantly Evolving

By 2017, according to the projection by **_comScore_**, Inc., 90.1 percent of the global online population will be accessing the internet from mobile phones. You know why? Because we want what we want, when we want it—and we want it *now*. This is the land of instant gratification!

To prove that, comScore states that 2014 was the first year that mobile usage exceeded desktop PC usage. Personally, I believe this is because our mobile devices are with us at all times. And because our devices are with us all the time, this will shift the way we make decisions.

Internet access will continue to become faster, and companies will continue to offer more data in an effort to keep up, feeding into that instant gratification I mentioned above. So, if you want to be able to compete, you need to get on board!

On the flip side of this, because we as Internet users are accustomed to this instant gratification, we no longer want to wait long periods of time for our content to load. We don't want to do the "pinch-and-zoom" method anymore, either. We want our content accessible no matter where we are, and we want it quickly.

To cater to that need, more businesses are investing in a mobile presence. Huge companies like Verizon and AT&T, as well as small businesses, are making mobile versions of their websites. It's the way things are going, and as I mentioned, if you want to compete...all aboard!

It's interesting how quickly our mobile devices have become the command center for a large chunk of our daily transactions. (Thank you, *__Apple Pay__* and Google Wallet!) With the touch of a few keys, we have access to our banking and billing information, and so much more. Eventually, *all* transactions will use one form of mobile device or another.

Mobile Mainstream

The more mainstream mobile presence becomes, the more you need to invest in it. The great news is that it's *really* easy to get started with that!

The easiest way to get a mobile site is to use a "responsive design." So what is a responsive design, you ask? In short, it's one website that uses the latest technology to adapt to screen size, whether that screen is on a desktop, tablet, or smartphone - even a TV.

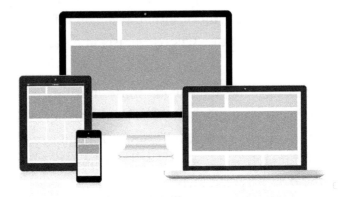

Because mobile devices are so mainstream, a majority of websites are now built using a responsive design. The benefits are huge, and once your site is complete, you'll wonder why other sites haven't converted.

The benefits for your site are numerous:

- You only have one site to manage content for. Years ago, mobile sites used a two-site system. This equalled double the work. If you needed to make an update or change to one site, you had to manually do it on the other as well. That wasted a lot of time. Responsive design eliminates this.

- A responsive design uses the same domain name, not a different domain name or subdomain such as m.example.com. No more javascript redirection!

- Responsive design uses the same design and branding as your desktop site.

- All you have to do is swipe, scroll, and touch to

get the information you're looking for, rather than the unfriendly "pinch-and-zoom" browsing I mentioned earlier.

- When people share a link to your website or the pages on it, the link will work on all devices. Responsive design simply responds to the device.

What If My Current Site *Isn't* a Responsive Design?

Most sites can be rebuilt to integrate these new responsive benefits without the need to scrap your site entirely, but any website created from now on *should* be built around a responsive design, especially if you want to be a front-running contender against your online competition.

> **A Little Piece of Advice:** Should you find that your web designer doesn't know about responsive design, find someone else. It's harsh, I know, but it's not easy!
>
> Mvestor Media can help! *mvestormedia.com*

What Makes Responsive Design So Great?

At Mvestor Media, we approach every design by starting with a mobile-friendly responsive design. Clever, right?

With each new client, we start with the smartphone version of a website, as opposed to a bigger version, and here's why:

- When dealing with a smaller screen, it forces the designer, and you as the site owner, to get rid of any content that isn't *absolutely* necessary. It's cutting out the "fluff" (crap).

- It forces you to think about the message you want to send—*what* is it that you do, make, or sell.

  - Another important thing to keep in mind is the need for a tagline. Website readers are "skimmers." They don't actually read every single word on every single website. They skim the page. They look for things that catch the eye. Like a tagline—your message, loud and clear at the top!

- When you're working with a screen the size of a smartphone, it really makes you prioritize what you want "***above the fold***," as well as acknowledge the content that is not as important, which you'll put at the bottom, keeping in mind your visitors' "skimming" habits. You don't have the usual space of a 22-inch monitor to work with.

- Based on the statistics I mentioned at the beginning of this chapter, you will get more use out of the mobile version of the site. You can't go wrong starting with a small mobile site. It really is a win-win.

> **Tip:** How to Know if a Site is Responsive. A super easy way to see if a site is responsive is to resize your web browser window. If the content adapts to the screen size, you have yourself a responsive site!

Time to Visualize: Is It Too Much? Will It Work?

Okay, so now that you understand why you need to have a mobile site, it's time to apply the knowledge you soaked up from **_chapter 1_**.

Imagine your mobile site as your *primary* site, not a condensed version of it. By doing so, you avoid the conundrum of trying to cram all your content into a tiny little device. If you design your mobile site as your primary site, desktops and tablets will show the *expanded* version of your website. And the benefits of this are endless!

How Do You Do That, Exactly?

In order to make this work, you start small and think bigger! Remember—easy to skim, easy to digest. Keep the scrolling to a minimum. Endless scrolling gets annoying. Prioritize your content, weigh its value, and then keep your content relevant.

Imagine the content you want on your site and ask yourself, "Does this content *need* to be on this page? Could I summarize this content and then offer a clickable link, should my visitors want additional information?"

When you do this, you create an easier-to-digest page without meaningless details, and you increase the positive experience your visitors are going to have.

Don't Make Them Think!

Here are a few best practices that you should keep in mind!

Phone and Address

Keep your phone number and address "above the fold." Make them large and at the top. This eliminates endless scrolling to find them. Remember our discussion in _**chapter 1**_ about not "hiding" from your visitors or clients.

The good news is, many mobile platforms today, such as Apple's iOS, will automatically make a company's number and address into clickable links. (Making your contact info into a clickable link is also something your web designer can and _should_ know how to do!) Your visitors' phones can dial the number for them and even add the address to the map or email application. The link with your contact information can also open into an email application. You can choose how your clients contact you. Just make it

THINK MOBILE: IT'S WHERE IT'S AT

simple, and don't make your users think!

Contact Forms

Next up are those pesky contact forms. Make them easy, and keep them short. Usually a name, email, and phone number are enough, and basically all the information anyone wants to give up anyway.

Should you need additional information, give visitors preselected options, rather than a text field. An empty text field makes them think. They don't like to think, remember? *We are lazy skimmers!*

You can keep it simple with a checkbox or a radio button for things clients might be interested in, rather than a text box that requires them to write a three-paragraph message. Make the checkboxes and radio buttons easy to tap, though!

For example:

I have questions about

- ☐ your hours
- ☐ your location
- ☐ your shipping rates
- ☐ your pricing

These pre selected "tap" options are a great way to keep people on your site. If visitors are required to type too much, they will most likely abandon your site.

Content Placement

I know I've already hammered this into your head, but as a friendly reminder, put your most important content up at the top of *every* page.

Mobile Content

If you think you want some content on the desktop version of your home page, but not on the mobile version, then it probably doesn't need to be on either. Don't take away content from your mobile design. We also need to leave the mindset that there are two versions (mobile and desktop), but instead, realize that there is only one responsive version. Make all content accessible on all screen sizes, or get rid of it.

Images

The number of images you have on each page will either make or break your load times. Be conscious of the images on each page. If your images take too long to load, users will abandon your site. Remember, we want what we want, and we want it right now!

Content Mix

To keep your visitors engaged, it's great to mix up your content with text, image, and video. One piece of advice when using video: *never* have auto-play videos. They're annoying, and they frustrate your visitors. Trust me. Don't do it... here's why: ***www.punkchip. com/autoplay-is-bad-for-all-users***

For faster videos, use a video hosting service like YouTube, Vimeo, or Wistia (my favorite.) These video hosting sites will allow your site's content to load before your video content, so if your visitors choose not to play a video, it won't delay your site's content from loading.

> **Bonus:** Transcribe or summarize your videos. That way your visitors can still get the value out of them without having to play them. This is good for visitors who may not have video playback capabilities, or maybe they're at work or church and don't want to blast the video content for everyone to hear. There's also bonus content for search engines. Hey, it happens. Don't judge!

Let's Wrap This Fat Chapter Up!

I know, that was a lot to digest, but trust me—this chapter has everything to do with the success of your website!

If you take nothing else from it, I hope you at *least* take this:

- *Start* with Mobile—usage will only become more widespread, and starting with a mobile site will help you prioritize your content.

- Remember, in 2014, 79.1 percent of the global

online population accessed the internet from mobile phones, and by 2017, that number is estimated to climb to 90.1 percent!

Inside your Website Worksheet, write down a few websites that have an easy and intuitive mobile and desktop website.

Chapter 5

Design: The Best Investment You'll Make?

Mistake: Designing a website that looks good, but isn't functional.

"Design is not just what it look like and feel like. Design is how it works."

If you take business advice from anyone, it might as well be Steve Jobs, right?

Design is *everything*. It's your website's "first impression," and you want that first impression to be a successful one! When you open up a site that has killer design, you instantly feel comfortable. More on comfortability is coming up.

First, keep the focus of your design dedicated to your visitors' experience. Doing so will ensure they stay on your site longer, dig deeper into what your site offers, and possibly become more qualified leads. All of that, just based on design alone. Crazy, right?

So how do you know if your design is giving a great first impression? Two ways:

- **Design Done Right** - When design is done right, you almost don't notice it. Your focus is on the content itself. When you *do* notice a design, it's because it's bad in some cases, and probably not created with the user in mind. Kind of a catch-22, really. Your design should be so good nobody notices it.

- **Design with Proper Balance** - This includes colors, images, alignment, spacing, typography, and so on. A proper balance will encompass all those things and make your site easy to navigate.

Your main focus is your customers or clients, right? So you want to balance your site appropriately. Envision how you want them to feel while on your site. Here's where comfortability comes into play.

When your customers are comfortable, they subconsciously assume a variety of things. If you have a great design, people assume you're legitimate. If you're legitimate, people will want to do business with you.

People spend their time and money where they feel comfortable, and companies that invest in great design, especially in all areas of marketing, are more likely to have loyal customers who spend more.

Prove It!

Think about the majority of successful companies...like Apple, for instance. How does Apple's design affect your willingness to buy? Apple invests a vast amount of time and money in design. Design in marketing, products, delivery...in *everything*.

And let's be honest, Apple basically controls the world. It also has an advantage because until recently, the marginal competition was relatively low, and companies are still hard-pressed to create things that can measure up to Apple's designs.

In the U.S., 51 percent of households own at *least* one Apple product, according to CNBC's All-America Economic Survey.

Another great example is the ***Dollar Shave Club***. Have you heard of it? The competition is rather steep, in my opinion, with the likes of Gillette and Schick, especially because those names have been around for years.

What gives Dollar Shave Club an edge against these big names? One reason—phenomenal design, from the website to the product packaging and even down to the handle of each razor. The website makes you feel comfortable, and it offers a great visitor experience. Go ahead and check it out. It's pretty phenomenal.

Another example, **_Mint.com_**. Their design is so good it makes users feel comfortable enough to hand over bank information to them, no joke.

Just Because It Looks Good Doesn't Mean It *Is* Good.

I've stressed the importance of design a lot in this chapter, but I also want to touch on an equally important aspect: functionality.

In order for design to be successful, it has to balance with functionality. Both need to work together to provide your visitors control. If the user doesn't have functional control, the design might as well look bad. Make sure that the design of your site doesn't contradict the "visitors first" principles I discussed in **_chapter 3_**.

Relaying What You've Learned to Your Designer

Web designers are great at what they do, but they are not mind readers. Communication is key! When you hire a designer, I recommend providing examples of what you're looking for. Your designer can better understand the ideas you have rattling around in your mind if you show a few visual examples of what you want. This opens up lines of feedback between you and your designer, and it also gives the designer a clearer idea of exactly what you're asking for.

You can refine your ideas in a couple of different ways:

- **Look at your competitors.** Think big, on a national and international scale, even if you only compete locally. Only focusing on your local competitors is going to limit your design potential, especially if your competitors' web designs aren't that great. You want to be the best of the best, and the possibilities are endless!

- **Be specific!** Tell your designer _**exactly what you like**_ about a website. For example, "I like the menu here," or "I like the large images." The more detail you give your designer, the better equipped he or she will be to design a website that you love!

- **Keep it simple and mobile.** As we discussed in the _**last chapter**_, your site should be responsive. When you do this, you purge the unnecessary content, which follows the simpler = better rule.

Trending Right Now: Flat

- flat design
- flat colors
- flat user experience
- flat user interface
- big text
- large images

- **Ask your designer's opinion.** If you are having trouble finding websites that you want to reference, ask your potential design team to send *you* examples of what *they* would recommend. That's why you're hiring them! Deciding on the look and feel of your website can be a collaborative process. Also, have them give you feedback on your feedback. Make sure what you are asking for is in your own self interest.

- **Avoid templates.** Choosing a template and running with it is a bad idea. Templates are created as a one-size-fits-all design to fit *any* business, but they don't have the ability to specialize. Templates will typically come with a bunch of features you won't want to use, sacrificing page speed and efficiency. Templates are good for getting **inspiration and trending ideas only.** Look but don't touch! You want someone with expertise to give you a personalized and hand-tuned design!

There Is Always Going to Be a Bias. How Do You Avoid a Bias Mistake?

A good design team can merge taste and culture perfectly. They are qualified to do what they do best, so let them!

I understand that every design comes with a personal bias: from you, from your family and friends, and even from your designer! Everyone has a specific taste, especially business owners. The problem with this is that you end up micromanaging every detail and designing your site for yourself, and not for the users.

The key is for your designer to be able to grasp your personal taste and businesses culture and articulately mesh them together with user experience and current trends. Professional web designers are qualified to do just that. If you need to get an opinion, get a qualified one. Your mom doesn't qualify, unless of course she is a professional web designer—and then by all means, ask her!

You want a site that you *and* your customers are going to like, so use your buyer personas to help dictate the design—and remember, you are not a web design expert. If you were, you wouldn't be reading this book. Neither is your spouse. I know that hurts, but you hired a design team for a reason!

Just ask yourself, would you like to have a site that *you* like, or do you want a site that your *customers* will like?

Make It Look Good *and* Be Good!

As we wrap this chapter up, I have a few best practices I want you to keep in mind.

- **Think mobile.** It really is the way to go, trust me. See the previous chapter.

- **Don't overemphasize your logo.** People visiting your site *will* see your logo; there is no need to make it gigantic. It becomes a distraction. Unfortunately, users don't care about your logo; they care about what you can *do* for them.

- **Showcase your affiliations.** Ask your designer where and how to incorporate your awards or the fact that you're a chamber of commerce member.

- Above all, **be consistent!**
    - Keep navigation in one place.
    - Keep information in one place and accessible.
    - Keep your button colors the same.
    - Stay consistent with your existing branding and marketing, especially in your printed materials. (Unless you're completely rebranding.)

Image Resources

It's important when designing your website that you use original or high-quality stock images to portray your message. Here are a few sights I recommend:

- Shutterstock.com - paid

- Fotolia.com - paid

- istockphoto - paid

- Creative Commons Image Search - free with attribution - **_search.creativecommons.org_**

Resources for design inspiration:

I look at these before every project to get my juices flowing. Business owners should do the same to get an idea for their site.

- The best of the best, literally award winning. **_www.awwwards.com_**

- Templates (good to see what's trending) **_themeforest.net_**

- WordPress showcase - **_wordpress.org/ showcase_**

Use the Website Worksheet to write down some websites that you like the design of.

Chapter 6

We All Want It: Control

Mistake: Taking away user control

As we've discussed in previous chapters, complete control provides users with a good experience. Following the "don't make me think" paradigm and the "visitors first" mentality, we are able to give users exactly that—control.

Two things provide users with complete control: design and functionality. Design, which I detailed in the last chapter, has to merge coherently with functionality in order to bring users the control they need and the experience they want.

Functionality can best be described as the way your website operates. When users hover over a button or visit a certain page and something happens, that is functionality. It's how your site works behind the scenes. When you combine design and functionality, you create "user experience."

User experience is how your user (mentally) experiences the design and functionality of your site. Users have high expectations. When they click on a "take me home" button or tab, and it takes them to a "services" page, you have taken away their control.

At all costs, you want to keep users from abandoning your site altogether, but now they have to think..."Did I click the wrong tab?" This can result in lost visitors, leads, and potential money. Make sense?

Things to Think about When Making Requests to Your Designer

In order to get a website that provides excellent user experience, you have to think like a user. It may sound like common sense, but ask yourself, how many websites do you visit each day that *could* offer a better user experience?

When designing your own website, ask yourself these questions:

- Can users find answers to their questions?
- Is it easy to navigate between pages?
- Are there places in the design that may confuse visitors?
- Can visitors find what they are looking for?

I've talked a lot about user experience, which is slightly different then my next point: user interface. User interface is what users use while having their experience. This encompasses the layout of the page and the design of your site. It's easy to make your interface look great, but is it easy to use? If it's not easy to use, it won't be used at all; and if it's not being used, it's because users don't have control.

So How Do I Give Users Control?

Back in the day, users would sacrifice interface usability for the sake of having new technology—the most animated, flashy technology that existed. People thought if their company's websites had those things, users would assume the company had money and was the real deal. It must have worked since we got this far with the internet.

Fast forward to today's websites. Now, users are all about usability. There are hundreds of places to buy product online. So people go where it is easiest to do it. Hello, buy with one-click-Amazon. People have figured this out and have since invested millions of dollars to design (or redesign) their companies' sites to be more user friendly. Sites no longer have over-done animations and flickering, sparkly marquee text. The technique of distracting users from doing what they came to do is a thing of the past. Animations used to be fancy and cool, but they also slow down your site, and in today's instant-gratification world, a slow website will not be tolerated.

Giving Users Complete Control: 4 Easy Steps

It's easier than you might think—giving your users complete control doesn't mean your site design will suffer. In fact, it will ensure your users have a great experience while on your site and hopefully come back again and again!

Here are a few specific things to avoid when designing your site.

#1: Auto-Play Videos

Auto-play videos are just a bad idea all the way around. Same goes for auto-play music. Think of your users—while surfing your site, they could be at work or even in bed while their partners are sleeping. This is more of a courtesy practice I recommend. You don't want to "out" your users when they're surfing your site discreetly, or trying to. Also, not everyone rocks a set of headphones all day. In case you missed it, check out this link:

www.punkchip.com/autoplay-is-bad-for-all-users

Automatically playing your video will not make your users want to watch it. It will, however, make them want to abandon your site—especially if they can't figure out how to turn it off. If your video catches your users' attention, and they're in a place that allows them to experience it, they will. W3C, the guys who control and set the standards for the web, say it's a no-no; and they wouldn't just say that unless they didn't have statistical backing to prove it.

#2: Pop-Ups: Everyone Hates Them, Trust Me.

Pop-ups that are generated on your own site are tools to get the user to opt in to something like a company newsletter. They are usually tied to a behind-the-scenes timer and automatically pop up once the user has been on any particular page for a certain amount of time.

But those pop-ups interrupt your users, which offends them. Repeat visitors or customers who were simply on the site to read a recent blog post and were interrupted by your pop-up will most likely exit the page entirely. I know I do. You took away their control by throwing a pop-up at them and making them lose their place while reading.

We all want to believe our company's newsletter is spectacular enough that *everybody* would want to opt in to it, but I recommend placing the newsletter opt-in on your site's sidebar, where it's not covering the users' field of view or interrupting them during their experience. There are also other, less intrusive ways to invoke action.

Examples:

HelloBar - *www.hellobar.com*

Small bar that stays fixed on the screen, at the top, out of your way. It's noticeable, but not in your face. Example at: *old.hellobar.com*

Corner Pop Ups - *sumome.com*

One of the many user experience tools at SumoMe, this corner pop up doesn't pop up mid screen, but typically in the bottom left or right-hand corner. Although bigger than HelloBar, you can still scroll without the notice being in your way.

In addition, consider using calls-to-action (CTAs) at the bottom of your blog posts or pages. Whatever you choose, keep it clear, direct, and concise. Use good design to make them stand out from the normal page flow, but no need to shove it in your visitors' faces.

#3: Long Website Forms: The Bane of Our Existence.

Nearly every website has them, and nearly everyone hates filling them out...but, if formulated correctly, forms can be a great tool to measure your site's productivity and user experience. Save the long forms for new customer intake forms, which allow you to collect a lot of information from a customer, but saves them time over sending and organizing it in an email. Win Win!

First, keep in mind the mobile site perspective, and keep the forms as short as possible. Even if your site isn't mobile-oriented (in which case you should fix that immediately), your forms still need to be short. Collect only the information that is necessary. Users are lazy, remember.

Another good practice is to make those radio buttons and checkboxes easy to tap, on a phone. The small box or circle is difficult to tap. Make them big!

You still want your users to have a great experience on your site, regardless of what they're doing! What you don't want is for your users to equate their "form experience" with their overall site experience, even after you've closed the deal.

As much as users hate to fill them out, sometimes longer forms are important to your company. If that's the case, make it clear ahead of time that the form your user is about to fill out is going to be a multi-page form or a specific number of questions. I recommend using a progress indicator in these instances. This allows users the control of seeing how close to completion they are. They like that.

I also recommend switching up your form terminology. Rather than using the word "submit" at the bottom, use the phrase "next page." This automatically tells your users they can expect more.

In summary, trim the form as much as you can!

#4: Tricky Business!

Don't try to trick or deceive your users. It will always backfire on you. Outside of your users' experience within your site, don't trick them into receiving things you never gave them the chance to opt out of—things such as company emails, e-newsletters, sales ads, and so on.

When you use information provided by your users for unsolicited opt-ins, it's technically against the law. It's known as the ***CAN-SPAM Act***. Per the CAN-SPAM Act website, "The CAN-SPAM Act establishes requirements for commercial messages, gives recipients the right to have you stop emailing them, and spells out tough penalties for violations."

If your users want to opt in for your company materials, they will. Make it easy for them by providing an opt-in checkbox at the bottom of forms not related to newsletters.

Common Sense...Er, Maybe Not?

Good website design gives users what they want instantaneously. This keeps users from abandoning your site. Think about your browsing experience. Would you abandon a site based on the things we talked about above? Ask yourself, what turns you off? Are your users getting what they're looking for? Is the result what the user expected?

What Other Ways Can Visitors Get a Hold of You?

Don't limit the ways in which your users can and will get a hold of you. Great company repoire involves your customers the ability to contact you in various ways, it is the 21st century, after all.

Unless you've lived under a rock, social media has exploded onto the interwebs, in recent years. It has also become a great tool for users to get in contact with a specific company and even a specific person, hello Twitter! Facebook and Google+ are littered (in a good way) with company profiles that will help connect users with the right people at lightening speed. And because companies are conscious about visitor/customer experience and positive feedback, they make a concerted effort to engage with their audience on every level.

I recommend you add social media icons in your design as a quick way for customers to find and engage with you! This can help you build a long term following.

Use the Website Worksheet to come up with a plan for giving users a good experience and control.

Chapter 7

Your Message: Make It Great; Make It Stand Out

Mistake: Conveying an unclear, boring message.

Let's be honest—at least a handful of times each day, you come across a website that really stands out, but you walk away with no idea of what it's actually trying to sell or do.

What's the point?

Why spend money making sure your website has fantastic design, is built around user experience, and loads quickly, but doesn't clearly convey your message?

In this chapter, I want to focus on taking the right

steps to make your message stand out and make a difference, so be prepared to take notes!

There Should Be Zero Question. Period.

Upon first loading your site, without scrolling, your visitors should know instantaneously what your business is about. If your website doesn't convey this, you've wasted your time and money—not to mention your developer's time.

So, how do you go about doing this? Simple. Say everything your company does, in ten words or less. For example, Mvestor Media's tagline is: "We build your website. You grow your business." It's extraordinarily simple, but without question, you know what my company does.

As simple as that tagline may be, it strongly suggests that we do more than *just* design websites. There are plenty of businesses that just do websites, so how does our tagline set us apart? Our message immediately sets the expectation that we are different from the rest. Not only do we design your website, but the second part of our tagline implies a myriad of other opportunities—mainly, the value associated with our services. That value could mean we are simply freeing up your time to grow your business or that we are providing resources to grow your business.

Here are some additional examples of major

companies and their headlines and tagline, at the time of this writing:

Base CRM: "Sales Teams That Use Base Sell More"
www.getbase.com

As a business owner, that headline, which is the first thing I see when I visit their site, tells me what problems they solve. If a sales manager is looking at this, they would be immediately captivated to explore the website to see *how* this is possible. This headline makes more sense than "Sales CRM" or "A CRM of Sales People". I can think of multiple CRMs - Highrise, Salesforce, Zoho, etc., so Base sets themselves apart.

Evernote: "Your Life's Work"
www.evernote.com

I love this headline! This is so much better than "Note taking software". Evernote helps anyone digitally inclined to "Remember Everything" (one of their previous taglines) by providing easy to use cloud software for note taking and archiving.

Any.do: "Get Things Done Like A Pro"
www.any.do

Again, this is better than "Task list manager". Pen and paper is a task list manager, so what separates Any.do from pen and paper? This headline makes me want to find out.

It really boils down to the message you want to send, as opposed to what it is you sell. So now that we've stated the importance of having a clear and direct message, let's jump into the difference between commodity and product.

Commodity Versus Product: Message Differences

Michael Gerber wrote a book titled *The E-Myth* that I think everyone in a business role should read. I was struck by the contrast Mr. Gerber made between commodity and product. Mr. Gerber states that companies sell two versions of the same thing— commodity and product.

- Commodity - the basic thing your company sells, i.e. furniture or cameras

- Product - the result of what is being sold

I want you, as the business owner, to be able to clearly distinguish between the two.

Take, for example, a financial planner. His commodity is life insurance, but his product or message is financial security. He is selling something of value to you, not *just* a life insurance policy. Another example is someone who sells cameras. The camera itself is the commodity, but the valuable product she is trying to sell is, "We help you capture family moments." Which one would you rather buy?

Again, it's setting yourself apart and asking, "What is the message I'm trying to send?" Think about all the industries with boring commodities. When you envision their potential messages, it generates a whole new level of thinking.

Here are a few examples of what I'm talking about:

Commodity	Product
Accounting	Pay less to the IRS
Insurance	Financial viability or security
Websites	Online lead generators
Chiropractic Care	Pain relief
Mattresses	A good night's sleep
Vitamins	Long-term health

Whatever your passion is, you need to communicate it effectively through your message. Successful companies are selling products, not commodities—especially your competitors.

If you get into the frame of mind to sell your product instead of your commodity, your strategy will naturally follow the same principles as your design, user experience, and buyer personas.

Your Message, Outlook, and Goal

You should convey your outlook through your message and the design of your site. This comes down to culture and the different ways you look at a particular industry. If you're setting yourself apart from your competitors because you offer a different paradigm on the way something should work, you want it to be evident within your design. Take Dyson vacuum cleaners, for example. Dyson has a different outlook and paradigm than traditional vacuum cleaner companies. People at Dyson don't *just* sell vacuums. They sell innovation and convenience.

Condense.

I don't care if you sell a hundred different things. Combine your products and services into ten words or less. Sometimes, you sell your commodity rather than the product itself. If you are selling cameras, which would be your commodity, but your message or product is "We capture moments in time," you want to clear up any vagueness by using images or text in your design to clearly state that you sell cameras. Make your message painfully obvious by having your product visible on your site in some way, shape, or form.

After you've distilled your products or services down to ten words or less using a combination of product and commodity, place that message at the top of your home page. You want your visitors to know exactly what it is that you do. It needs to be the first thing they see!

Apply these principles to each of the page titles, as well. Make them compelling, less boring than the generic "About Us" or "Our Services" categories. Mix it up! Make it fun and engaging, but don't go overboard. Instead of "Contact Us," "Contact a Camera Genius" sounds much more appealing, right?

Practice Makes Perfect

In your Website Worksheet, write down what your products and commodities are. Now, come up with a few different main headline options that will be on your home page. Remember, keep them creative and relevant!

Chapter 8

You Want It? Ask For It!

Mistake: Not asking for what you want.

Asking for what you want is the best way to get it - leads, sales, newsletter sign-ups, prospects, free trial users, demo users, etc. It's no guarantee, though. And overcoming the psychology of asking can be tricky. In business and sales, more often than not, you must *ask* for the sale to happen. The same is true for gaining leads and making sales through your website.

Staying consistent to what we've discussed in previous chapters, you must *ask* for your users to do things, instead of tricking them or taking away their control. You want them to sign up for your newsletter? Ask them. When you ask them for their information, you are implying that they will get something in return. Nothing in life is free, even an eNewsletter.

Remember, your visitors are looking for something that your website will hopefully provide, whether that be a product, a service, or a solution to their problems. Make it painfully clear to them so they know what they're getting and what they need to give up to get it.

Ask for the Yes!

A little beyond the scope of this book, but totally relevant, is the psychology behind asking for what we want. It's been said that the person who asks the questions controls the situation. This is also true in a sales-oriented business. The catch is that you have to ask the right questions. Questions help build trust and rapport, as well as enhance your credibility.

Many people don't ask for what they want simply because they are afraid of getting a "no." For example, if you're at a point where the next step is to close the sale, unless it's a home run, you have to ask for it (i.e., "Are you ready to sign up?").

Depending on where your visitors are in the sales cycle, you need to *ask* for things to happen. Obviously, you wouldn't ask for a sale from people who are still considering their options and gathering information. You wouldn't ask someone to sign a proposal you haven't given to them yet, either.

A majority of people who visit your site have already told you "no"; you just don't hear it, because they're not saying it to your face. Every person who comes to your site and doesn't buy something or fill out a lead generation form is a tentative "no."

When you scour your analytics, you will see that a lot of people tell you no. When you look at it across the board, it's a numbers game. A successful conversion rate can be 1 percent, because for every 100 visitors who land on your sales page, it would be a success if just one showed interest.

Direct—but Not Pushy

If you're more direct about what you want, it's entirely possible that you can turn that 1 percent into a greater number, without needing to increase your traffic. It really comes down to numbers. Your visitors have to know up front what you're asking of them, and then they can decide if the value of your offer is enticing enough.

It's important that you have an *offer* instead of just ambiguous phrases (i.e. "We can help you with xyz"). Have something your visitors will want (down-loadable content, for example) without pressuring them to *buy* anything. We touched briefly on the use of calls-to-action (CTAs) in **_chapter 1_**, so you should be familiar with the need for them to be relevant as well as provide a solution for your visitor's problem.

When you have good design, you build trust with your users. There are thousands of offers on various websites, and more times than not, people say no.

Why is that? Because there's a lack of trust. Design is important to build that trust, as well as to get your message out there.

Conclusion

Build your case with good solid copy and headlines. Ask your visitors to do something, in exchange for something else. Marketing comes into play here.

Test and try different variations of an offer. Ask your web developer to setup a "split test" or "A/B test". This is where you have a single offer, but change a minor, but effective element about it.

For example, let's say you want more newsletter sign ups. You can set up an offer on every page with the headline "Sign up for our newsletter" - test "A". A split test would entail changing the headline and serving that version to half of the visitors, test "B".

The version with more newsletter sign ups is the winner. You can continue to test this over and over, obtaining incrementally better results.

> Use the Website Worksheet to jot down what you want your visitors to do while on your site and how you might get them to do it.

Chapter 9

Compelling Content: Attractive and Effective Offers

Mistake: Delivering an unattractive, ineffective message.

In the two previous chapters, I discussed creating your message and gave you a slight introduction to calls-to-action (CTAs). In this chapter, I want to discuss delivering your message and creating attractive offers, content, and CTAs. In order to accomplish this, you need to understand how people navigate and read content on the web.

Reading content on the web isn't the same as reading a book. We no longer read every word and line in front of us. We skim. We look for bits and pieces of intriguing content that will catch and keep our attention. We also look for answers to our questions or solutions to our problems. So don't force your visitors to read every line of your website, because they will most likely abandon your site.

Give them control and allow them to skim. It feeds the need for instant gratification. Visitors want to find what they want to find, and they want to find it right now. Giving your visitors what they want the way they want it will keep them on your site longer.

What Makes Good, Skimmable Content?

You need to provide easy-to-digest content in a straightforward format. Sounds easy enough, right? So how do you format your content to achieve that?

Break up your copy using compelling, eye-catching headlines.

- While on the web, people typically skim content instead of reading it like a book.
- Use creative wording that summarizes the following paragraph. If the headline catches visitors' attention, they're more likely to continue reading.

Use bulleted lists and points.

- They're easy to read.

- They're easy to summarize.

- They break up your text.

- They drive home your main point(s).

Use visuals—the possibilities are endless.

You can use pictures, charts, graphs, interactive designs, videos, and so on. (Don't auto-play sound!) Visuals make your content easy to skim!

- A picture is worth a thousand words.

- Images allow you to show emotion that supports your main body, headlines, and subheads.

K.I.S.S.

- Simply put, "Keep it simple, stupid." (See what I did there?)

- Why use ten words when you could use seven? Less is definitely more.

The Hierarchy of Content

Believe it or not, content really does have a hierarchy. Some content belongs above the fold, while other content does not. Then there's the content that should just be tossed.

So how do you decide which content you need to keep and which content should be tossed?

Keep this content:

- answers to your buyer personas' questions
- frequently asked questions, in general or per product or service level
- case studies about particular clients and services
- information about how you work
- the process and systems you use that set you apart from your competition

Written Content Best Practice

Here is a summary that lays out the best practices for your written content:

- Break up your copy using headlines, bullets, and imagery.
- Write clear and concise copy that directly answers your visitors' questions
- Keep it simple; don't get too wordy. People hate wordy.

Use Various Forms of Content to Generate Leads:

Videos are convenient and easy. Your visitors don't have to skim! They can sit back in their chairs while the information is fed to them. But keep in mind, not everyone has the capability to watch videos on their phones (think mobile), so don't depend solely on videos. You can transcribe your videos into text, which can then be broken down using headlines and bullets to make it compelling! There's a great company called SpeechPad that transcribes videos; check it out.

You can also use:

- whitepapers
- eBooks
- memberships
- books
- presentations
- recordings/podcasts

The types of content you can offer are unlimited! But, because these other, more "premium" types of content can be fairly expensive, I recommend developing your CTAs first. With these other forms of content, you're usually offering knowledge that you would normally be paid for—that's OK, the clients don't *have* to hire you, but make them into leads *before* they get access to that type of content.

Using Your Awesome Content for a CTA

Once you have your premium content, such as an eBook, create a clear offer that asks for *something*. (Remember to stay consistent with everything we've covered in previous chapters.)

So, how should you do that? I have found great

success placing a CTA at the bottom or on the sidebar of blog posts and service pages. The main thing to remember is to *stay on topic*. If you waver off topic, your CTA becomes irrelevant.

Make your CTA title very clear: "How to Get 7 New Patients This Month." That title provides a clear understanding of what you're getting if you click on it.

Also, remember to be up-front about what the user will need to give in order to get what you're offering. When users respond to your CTAs, you can deliver your promised content via email, in addition to a "thank you" page that allows your users to immediately access it. Be sure to collect information that feeds directly into a CRM or database of leads and prospects.

Multiple CTAs

Different CTAs should be used for prospects who are in different stages of the buying process. Someone who is closer to buying (looking at pricing, on a free trial, etc) is probably more apt to answer an email or phone call from you, compared to a person who just discovered what your product is. They may not even know they need your product yet, so be careful when reaching out to prospects, as they may consider it to be too pushy.

Thank You Pages

Sincerely thank your visitor for signing up to receive your content. **Clearly state how they will receive it, whether it will be via email or direct download.**

> **Pro Tip:** Include your Facebook Like Box or Twitter Follow Button on thank you pages. These visitors are engaging with you more than your average visitor, so take advantage of it and prompt them to follow you on social media.

Pay with a Tweet

You should also consider tech-nologies such as Pay with A Tweet or Pay with a Like where you will give a visitor the content in exchange for a Tweet about it. This can generate  more opt ins for your content and has the potential to go viral.

The Bottom Line?

Keep it simple, make it clear, and mix it up! Also, think about your prospects and what stage of the "buyer's journey" they are in. Someone who is ready to buy a product now will respond to a stronger CTA or sales copy than someone who doesn't even know they need your product yet.

| Use the Website Worksheet to come up with different pieces of content for potential visitors.

Chapter 10

Content Management

Mistake: Not utilizing a CMS.

Any site that is built today should be built using a Content Management System (CMS). A CMS is software that runs your website; it allows you to edit your own website without needing to understand programming languages like HTML and CSS. (That is something you're paying your developer to understand.) Using a CMS is a way for you, or any developer for that matter, to easily add necessary updates down the road, without it being a costly process.

CMS Benefits

There are multiple benefits to using a CMS. In today's modern age, there are rarely reasons not to use a CMS. Some benefits include:

Page Templates

A CMS allows the use of page templates (not to be confused with design templates). Templates can be used over and over for a multitude of pages. Change the template once, and all pages are updated. Any site that doesn't use a template or CMS would require each and every page to be changed individually. Over dozens to thousands of pages, this will become time consuming and costly.

Built by the Best

The best content management systems we have today typically have contributions from the best developers in the world. If the best-of-the-best are using them and contributing to them, so should you.

Security

Popular CMS's are often "patched" and updated to fix possible security holes in modern web technology. Having a CMS can allow you to receive updates and fixes to these security issues.

There are two major categories of CMS: open source and proprietary.

Open-Source CMS

Open-source content management systems—WordPress, Joomla, Drupal, and so on—are typically free, community-driven content platforms. Word-

Press is the most popular. An open-source system gives you a more "do-it-yourself" type of website.

There are many pros to using an open-source platform, one being the cost. Everyone loves free! You get the benefit of community-driven support, which means there are usually a lot of updates to the platform. It's compatible with a variety of web hosts. It's also independent, and by that I mean you don't have to worry about "upgrading" to the next plan if you want to grow your site. It's free, and as long as you have the knowledge to use it, it doesn't cost you a thing.

With every pro, there is always a con. The con here is that if something goes wrong with this type of platform, you're SOL. There is no official priority support. No email, live chat, or anything. Your only source of support would be your developer.

Proprietary CMS

A site that uses a proprietary CMS is very limited— Shopify, Bigcommerce, Wix, and Squarespace, for example.

Even though your options may be somewhat limited, these sites also have a few pros. Most notably, they're turnkey. Give the CMS company your credit card number, and within hours you have a site. Granted, it's a template site, but a site nonetheless. It's also low cost compared to developing a website.

Most often, this type of company acts as your website host as well.

The cons include the fact that you will be required to abide by the company's standards, which can be both good and bad. Your site will be created using generic templates, so it won't be original; there's a chance you'll find a hundred other websites that look just like yours. Your features will be limited, and until the majority of people using the platform request a certain feature, chances are, the company won't add it to the mix.

You cannot customize a proprietary CMS as much as an open-source CMS. And with a proprietary CMS, you can't take your website and move it to another platform. *Your* content is actually *theirs* and is held hostage, if you will. And unless the company has a "data liberation" agreement or something similar, you lose your site entirely if you cancel.

My Professional Opinion

I, personally, as well as my company, Mvestor Media, stand behind using an open-source, community-driven CMS. Specifically, WordPress. Why? Because it allows us to create the website and turn it over to you.

According to ManageWP, 74.6 million sites depend

on WordPress. "In the realm of self-hosted sites, WordPress accounts for 18.9 percent of all websites."

That may not seem like a lot, but given the myriad of content management systems out there, and the fact that 70 percent of sites worldwide *do not use a CMS*, that's pretty astounding.

Additionally, as of the time of this writing, according to BuiltWith Trends (***trends.builtwith. com/cms***), WordPress accounts for:

- 49.3% of the top 10,000 sites on the internet

- 49.4% of the top 100,000 sites on the internet

- 51.93 of the top 1,000,000 sites on the internet

WordPress has proven to be not only the easiest, but the most popular.

The other thing I really love about WordPress is that it allows you to edit your site's source code to your personal liking, and it can be used for virtually any type of website—forums, informational, business, eCommerce, membership, even social networking.

And if you don't want to do the editing, it makes it easy for us to handle that, and your long-term maintenance cost will be lower. Creating something that is easy to use is going to be cheaper for you, as the client.

To Wrap Up

Save yourself a lot of time and heartache by

choosing the right CMS for your site. What is going to save you time, money, and effort in the long run? You want something easy, efficient, and reliable.

> Use the Website Worksheet to determine what areas of your site might change often that you would want to manipulate?

Chapter 11

Hosting: Your Site Alive

Mistake: Cutting costs using a cheap web hosting.

What is hosting, exactly? A web host is the service that provides space on the Internet for your website. If you want your website to be seen by others, you will need to publish it to a web hosting service.

There are literally hundreds of thousands of web hosting options to choose from. Web hosting has become more common thanks to the growing demand for it. Technology continues to evolve, and so will hosting sites.

For the here and now, I recommend adhering to the "three s" mnemonic for choosing a suitable hosting site: speed, security, and support. Ideally, you want to have all three key points.

Speed

Your visitors are impatient and looking for instant gratification, which we covered in chapter four. The speed of your site is a major factor. How much is a potential customer worth to you if he or she leaves your site because it doesn't load quickly enough?

If you're saving five dollars a month by using a cheap host that doesn't provide your site with an adequate load time, are you really saving anything? Not really. In fact, you're losing money when potential visitors abandon your site because it isn't loading quickly enough. I recommend looking at sites your potential web host keeps, so you can evaluate the speed of those sites before you sign up with the host. This will give you the opportunity to see how things work. Spend the money for a hosting site that won't cost you potential leads. The extra money each year is more than worth it.

Security

You want your hosting site to be able to provide the security of your site not getting hacked. It's that simple. You don't want to invest your time and money in a website that is at risk of being hacked because of a poor hosting site.

So how are they preventing a hack? *Are* they being proactive in preventing it from happening in the first place? It's not enough for the hosting site to have systems in place *if* a hack happens, but if it does, how are they going to rectify it?

Look for these things: Are they using antivirus, anti-malware software? Do they have a firewall?

Consider this: Cheap hosts' goal is simply numbers. The want to put as many paying customers onto a single server as possible. While their hardware costs will remain the same, they can turn more profit for each physical machine they build. By selling server space at a low cost, more customers will flock to it. This means your website will sit on the same server as hundreds to thousands of other websites.

Additionally, if even **one** of those sites gets hacked, there is the possibility that the site infection can move and infect your own website, despite the fact that you have your own unique password to your account. Since it sits on the same server, it is still possible. The good news is, there are methods of blocking this, so make sure you ask your host what they are doing to protect your site.

Lastly, how can you implement a backup system? Despite a company's best guard against a hack, nothing is foolproof. A backup system is paramount. So is testing your restores.

Support

In the event something happens, how reliable is the support of your hosting company? Can you pick up the phone and call them? Do they offer live chat or email?

Does the hosting company have any knowledge of your website type? Do they specialize or generalize in web technology? You can't be an expert on everything.

This is important, especially if for some unknown reason your site is "down." Is it going to take your hosting site three days to get back to you? This corresponds with using a "cheap" hosting site; it may not have the funds to prioritize, direct, and support your recovery.

In relation to the level of support your hosting site provides, there is also something known as an SLA.

Service-Level Agreement (SLA)

Each web hosting site has what is referred to as an "uptime" or service-level agreement (SLA). This equates to the percentage of time your website will be up and running properly, which is calculated each calendar month. For example, my company's host, WP Engine, has an SLA for 99.95 percent service availability. They guarantee that my site will be up and running 99.95 percent of the time, and for anything less than that, they will credit next month's bill. The hosting site you choose should hold itself accountable.

Cheap Hosting Doesn't Save You Money.

In a perfect world, you want to have all the things we discussed above *and* a cheap monthly bill, but it doesn't usually work like that. You rarely get speed and security without paying for it. Just remember, you get what you pay for, and when it comes to your website, cheaper isn't better.

Looking for recommendations?

I have them. These are loosely based on the type of website you will have.

By far, managed web hosting is the most valuable type of hosting available today. Managed web hosts typically take only one type of website. Our web host, WP Engine, takes only WordPress-based websites. By doing so, they're able to optimize their servers for speed, security, and support. At $29 per month for a single site (pricier than other hosting platforms), you make up for the cost in setup time and support.

Other examples of managed hosts include:

Synthesis—WordPress Hosting

Pantheon—WordPress and Drupal hosting

JoomlaWired—Joomla-dedicated hosting

Magenting—Magento-dedicated hosting

Remember, don't bend over a dollar to pick up a dime. Hosting your website is very important, so a host that will address your concerns, as well as operate your site and bring you peace of mind, is worth its weight in gold.

Use the Website Worksheet to determine the important factors of web hosting for your business.

Conclusion

Thank you for taking this journey with me! The information in this book is a collection of the ideas and experiences of myself and my team at Mvestor Media. Our goal at Mvestor Media is to allow you to grow your business. Our tagline, We Build Your Website, You Grow Your Business is what we live by.

We can all make the web a better place by following the principles in this book. Designing your site is not just about what colors or patterns to use, it's about providing your visitors what they are looking for.

If you can do that effectively, you'll be on the right track to gaining more business through your website!

> **BONUS:** For reaching the end of the book, you get a bonus! Send a copy of your completed Website Worksheet to me for a free gift:
> *book@mvestormedia.com*

www.ingramcontent.com/pod-product-compliance
Lightning Source LLC
LaVergne TN
LVHW022354060326
832902LV00022B/4440

* 9 7 8 1 5 1 7 0 0 5 6 3 4 *